DIANNA FUEMANA

Dianna Fuemana was born in Auckland. The youngest of her family, she has seven siblings who were born in Amerika Sāmoa and Niue.

In 1999 she was nominated in the Chapman Tripp Theatre Awards for Outstanding New Writer of the Year. That same year, her acclaimed play *Mapaki* was performed around New Zealand and then toured internationally across the United States and Athens, Greece.

Fuemana completed a Master of Creative and Performing Arts with Honours in 2005 at the University of Auckland, writing *The Packer* during her study. *The Packer* was performed in New Zealand and Australia as well as at the Edinburgh Fringe. *Falemalama* was produced during a residency in the United States in 2006 at the Pangea World Theater, Minneapolis.

Also a director, actor and producer, she was selected to attend the 10th Pacific Arts Festival in Pago Pago, Amerika Sāmoa with *Falemalama* in 2008. Ali Foa'i and Reid Falemalama Faith Elisaia performed the work in the village of Utulei. In the same year, she won the Pacific Innovation and Excellence Award at Creative New Zealand's Arts Pasifika Awards. Fuemana has played a leading role in the development of Pacific Island theatre in New Zealand.

ALSO BY DIANNA FUEMANA

Jingle Bells

Mapaki

My Mother Dreaming

TWO PLAYS
DIANNA FUEMANA

Play*market*
NEW ZEALAND'S PLAYWRIGHTS' AGENCY
& SCRIPT ADVISORY SERVICE
www.playmarket.org.nz

Copyright © 2008 Dianna Fuemana

First published in 2008 by Playmarket

Playmarket
Level 2, 16 Cambridge Terrace
Wellington, New Zealand

National Library of New Zealand Cataloguing-in-Publication Data
Fuemana, Dianna.
Two plays / Dianna Fuemana.
(New Zealand play series, 1178-2943)
ISBN 978-0-908607-32-7
I. Title. II. Series: New Zealand play series.
NZ822.3—dc 22

This book is copyright. Apart from fair dealing for the purpose of private study, research, criticism or review, as permitted under the Copyright Act, no part may be reproduced by any process without prior permission of the publisher.

The author asserts her moral rights in the work.
The production of this book was made possible by a generous contribution from Creative New Zealand and the New Zealand Players Trust.

Permission to perform these plays, and further copies from the New Zealand Play Series, may be obtained from Playmarket.
www.playmarket.org.nz

Cover design by Sorelle Cansino, Base Two, Wellington, New Zealand

Editorial supervision by John Huria, Ahi Text Solutions, Wellington, New Zealand

Typeset and project managed by Whitireia Publishing, Wellington, New Zealand

Printed and bound by Astra Print, Wellington, New Zealand

To Solomon and Reid

NEW ZEALAND PLAY SERIES

Three Plays Gary Henderson

Two Plays Toa Fraser

Two Plays Dianna Fuemana

Tzigane John Vakidis

The Daylight Atheist Tom Scott

ALSO PUBLISHED BY PLAYMARKET

He Reo Hou: Five Plays by Māori Playwrights
edited by Simon Garrett

Hot Tips for Hot Scripts
by Roger Hall

Playmarket New Zealand Theatrescripts Series
edited by David Carnegie

CONTENTS

FOREWORD	9
INTRODUCTION	13
THE PACKER	17
INTRODUCTION	45
FALEMALAMA	53

FOREWORD

With Auckland's bustling multicultural Karangahape Road as epicentre, in these two plays Dianna Fuemana provides a portrait of the world's largest Pacific Island city, and draws on her mother's story to describe one of the journeys that brought the Pacific to it. Both *The Packer* and *Falemalama* are full of familial separations and cultural dislocations, but, in finding the love, generosity and ambition of people determined to be themselves during periods of change, together they offer us hope for a strong Pacific future.

Playmarket's New Zealand Play Series sees the publication of major works for the stage. In the last 15 years New Zealand has produced many significant plays that have remained unpublished. This new series, which began in 2007 with the publication of plays by Gary Henderson and Toa Fraser, seeks to ensure significant titles reach the readership and further audiences they deserve, creating an essential body of New Zealand literature.

I'd like to acknowledge Creative New Zealand and the New Zealand Players Trust who have both contributed to the costs of producing the three titles Playmarket is publishing in 2008. Thanks are also due to our Foundation subscribers, listed at the back of this volume, who are helping ensure this series' continuance.

Playmarket is New Zealand's playwrights' agency and script development organisation. We not only license, develop, publish and promote plays, our online (www.playmarket.org.nz/bookshop) and in-house bookshop is a one-stop shop for those wishing to purchase New Zealand plays.

Mark Amery
Director, Playmarket

NEW ZEALAND PLAY SERIES PRESENTS

THE PACKER

"AN ABSOLUTE KNOCKOUT OF A SHOW... SHARP, FRENETIC & JAW ACHINGLY FUNNY" THE MELBOURNE TIMES

INTRODUCTION

2003. It was supposed to be the final year of my master's degree. It was a means to an end. I wanted to produce my plays because I felt that no one else would. My work is not that of the 'mainstream', so I wanted to learn business skills that would help me get money to take my work abroad, where the pool is bigger and ideas around 'what theatre is' are more vast than small-town Auckland with all its 'white' British- and American-produced plays. Problem was, I had just been told I could not finish my degree in what I had majored in, which was arts management. It was a major stress at the time and I remember almost giving up on it. My sister came to pick me up from uni and I couldn't even sit in the car. I jumped out at the lights and walked the ten kilometres from downtown Auckland to Avondale furious! It started to rain and thunder, and the angry tears started to flood. Then, a light bulb went off in my head and a voice said, 'Cross credit these points over to a theatre major and write a play supported by your favourite dramaturg, Dr Murray Edmond!' I'd already had a successful one-woman show and a three-hander comedy produced. It was the space I needed to just write, semi-supported by part-time jobs, a student allowance and generous mates who supported the glamorous side of life.

My final master's year began with my third play, *Licker*. It was a working title that reminded me to write something sexy this time round. I wanted to write something from my urban Auckland roots. I was raised in West Auckland so had a good ear for the dialogue and the eccentricities. I had a Palagi actor mate who was also from the West. I'd spent a lot of time with his family over the summer of 2003 and we were all hanging out in a holiday house at Piha Beach that we had rented. Funny, we didn't even get to the beach – it was one of those rainy Auckland summers. What stirred me as a writer during this window was the reflection of how similar in 'culture' we were, although we were people from two different ethnic backgrounds,

13

different upbringings and different lifestyles. Something made it really easy for us to connect. Was it the 'Westside?' I couldn't put my finger on it but liked that. I started playing around with the idea of 'Bright Niue Girl vs Dumb White Trash Boy' from West Auckland. I first thought that the story was going to be a political, rape drama story, but alas the title 'Licker' reminded me to stick with 'sexy, sassy and bright'. That's when the focus became a 'coming of age' theme. The same Palagi mate was cast in a popular Australian soap that was shooting in Melbourne. I thought, 'What a bonus! I'm writing a shit-hot one-man show, and I can use the 'soap star' status to promote a tour to the UK and Australia,' and then, POW! The prospect of *The Packer* was solidified on a bus home to Avondale. I realised the arts management studies did rub off.

I commuted from Auckland to Melbourne over the year to workshop the story with my Palagi mate who was the sole actor. Once I had finished the final draft I moved over for the rehearsal period and we rehearsed nights in a freezing cold preschool in the middle of a dodgy, drug-dealer infested park in Fitzroy. The laughter in that room was the only thing that kept me warm! We flew back to New Zealand and opened the show in Wellington at BATS Theatre. I remember sitting next to an actor who whispered to me during the show, 'What the fuck were you thinking, Dianna?' I got the feeling some people didn't quite know how to take the story ... Luckily, I'd had the experience of being able to stand up for my work so I gave him a sharp punch in the arm. He left quickly after the show. I think he was jealous that the 'white guy' got the 'black girl'. Good job! When we took it to the Edinburgh Festival it was a hit with the young black girls. They loved it! That meant a lot to me. I don't often see theatre that promotes the 'black girl' as the super smart, take-no-shit kind of person. Especially one who is pursued by a spunky 'white boy'.

How could I not explore where I'm from, what I know and what makes me laugh out loud? I couldn't. So I did, with the riveting talent of my Palagi mate, Jay Bunyan.

Dianna Fuemana
Auckland 2008

Original Production

First performed at BATS Theatre, Wellington, New Zealand
August 2003

with the following cast and creative team:

All characters were played by Jay Bunyan

Directed by Dianna Fuemana

Lighting design by Trygve Wakenshaw

Characters

SHANE: Kiwi, 23-year-old Auckland white-trash westie. Good looking with charm to burn. He's a ladies' man and a mean hip-hop rapper who looks after his alcoholic mother.

MUM: Australian, 40-year-old gin-wielding alcoholic who just keeps on pouring them. She has been diagnosed manic-depressive and is receiving the sickness benefit. She came to New Zealand on her OE and stayed on when she knew she was pregnant with Shane. Thick Australian outback accent.

PINA: Niue girl. Twenty-two years old and in the last year of her political science degree. She is gorgeous and intelligent and doesn't take shit from no one.

TALE: Pina's dad, 45 years old and an Island charmer. He is a ladies' man and a liberal father. Thick Niue accent.

BRAD: Kiwi, 22-year-old Auckland white-trash wigger. He is the ultimate white wigger wannabe, and is a closet homo.

CHARLENE: Auckland white-trash slut, 22 years old. She comes from a well-to-do family and relishes the opportunity to be with bad boys.

DIPTANSHU: Indian taxi driver who used to live next door to Shane and Mum until his wife realised he was having an affair with Shane's mum. He is nervous and has a thick accent.

QUEEN: Edinburgh Street transvestite hooker.

THE PACKER

The story is told in a box-packing factory. The set has a distinct industrial feel. Large reinforced cardboard boxes are used for furniture and the action of the piece.

There is pre-show music which is loud and funky. Once audience is in actor slowly comes out in blackout and begins to stack boxes as lights gradually fade up with humming sound of a factory ...

SCENE ONE

SHANE: There are approximately two hundred and twenty-four thousand bubbles in a ten-metre roll of bubble wrap. There are twelve folds in a box that needs erecting. I can stack three hundred boxes in an eight-hour day and five hundred and fifty-two on a double shift ... No, what am I talking about. It's two hundred and twenty-four thousand bubbles in a twelve-metre roll. There are definitely twelve folds in a box. Are there?

Pause.

I think about her nearly every minute of the day. Even when I don't think about her for a few minutes, I think, 'I haven't thought about her for the last minute'. I've woken up every morning feeling lost before the day even starts. My depression is the only thing that gets me to sleep, that and the pot, shit loads ... It's my first day back in a week and I'm on the double shift. I got this project I started recently. It was born from my broken arseness. Something to get into instead of the other shit.

Pause.

Last week, before I knocked off, I was thinking, save a bit, put a deposit on a car. Say, two grand. Pay it off, seventy bucks a week on HP over three years. Could get a sweet vehicle. Ford maybe.

Get some second-hand Trident mags even. And a sunroof too. Wind blowing on my hair.

Sugar honey pot, honey pot sniffing at my pits ... Sweet ... But that's all shit, aye. It's funny how some shit can change what you think in a blink of an eye. Your hopes. Your dreams. You just never know what's around the corner

Pause.

Fuck, I got home last Friday night, opened the front door, walked in, opened my bedroom door, threw my shit on the floor, sat on the bed with a bounce and switched on the box.

SCENE TWO

Lights change to SHANE's house.

SHANE: Mum, here's your gin, got a big night out tomorrow night. I'm crashing. I'll make you eggs tomorrow. Tea or coffee?

MUM: Well, it's gonna depend on how I feel in the morning isn't it, love. I'm not a mind-reader you know, if I knew what I wanted I'd tell ya, but if I had that power to begin with, gawd, I don't think I'd be here, not sure you would be either, come to think of it ... I probably wouldn't drink so much. I only started getting regular on it to cope with your teen years, Shane. You were a horrible adolescent. Thank gawd, I can hardly remember it!

SHANE: Exactly how many gins have you had tonight, Ma?

MUM: You know I got a bad habit for the gin, love. Especially the weekends. I get lonely on my own, Shane. Those fucken wankers at the social welfare office reduced my sickness benefit too, so I'm not at all feeling well, love. Make sure you save some of your pay for shopping next week. Don't blow it all on the weekend. And you can leave your board on the bench, too.

SHANE: Yeah, Ma. Easy on the gin and you'll get a better sleep aye. I got a big night out with Brad tomorrow night. Looks like I might get a chance to show some skills. (*aside*) And I don't want to be looking after your drunk ass.

MUM: What was that you said, love? You being cheeky, you little devil. Go on off to bed with you. Your Ma's all right. Shane, I love ya, love. You know that, don't ya.

MUM pours herself a gin, sits and sips. She hums 'Waltzing Matilda'. She pours another drink then gets up and paces the room drunk.

MUM: Could have visited me down here. Down under. Down under, down under. Family. Gawd. Only letters. Letters. I miss 'em. Ma, Pa, Sissy, still in rehab. Little brother still serving his time. Little bugger. Told him not to get involved with that lot. Wog mafia. They're a bloody force, they are. Oh, I'm lucky to have Shane. (*to God*) You hear that. Shane. Shane Johnson. My one and only. (*she sings*) Hopelessly devoted. Bless him! Not every one is born with the good looks. His father had the good looks. Luigi Marco ... Shhhshhhh. Blimey, almost let the cat out the bag. That fucken mafia.

She sits and falls asleep.

SCENE THREE

The lights change to show a night and morning has passed. It is now afternoon.

MUM: Shane ... Shane! You awake, love? Well you should be, it's just after three. All that noise woke me, I swear I'm gonna need another drink to get rid of this headache!

She rises, and goes over to the window and is peeking through the curtain spying on the new neighbours.

I think someone's moving in next door. I hope it's not bloody Indians like the last lot. That curry smell day in day out, really brought on my asthma, you know. Don't get me wrong, baby, I like the Indians. Got nothing against them but I wonder what goes on behind those tills and bindies. I reckon as long as they stay in those Bollywood films, I think they can be a real good example for their youth. Like *Bend it like Beckham* you know, those sort of Indians. Oh, Olivia Newton-John was my one. Loved her. Looked up to her, until she married that wog. Gawd, I loved growing up in Australia. Are you watching what's happening next door or are you fluffing round with your hair? Gawd, Shane I wonder sometimes, I really do with you.

SHANE: (*In bathroom, appears freshly woken. He goes for a piss then washes his face. He fingers his hair back.*) What you ranting on about. It all seems good. One man, and one chick.

He looks out the window.

Looks as if she could be his daughter. And a fine one at that. Gee, those island girls need their own music video, I swear. Shouldn't be a problem neighbour. Looks decent enough.

He practises a rap.

Pure and simple. Casanova? Obvious. One look? Is all it takes. Twice? And she didn't want you cause she never knew you. Three times? Leave the bar and move to a trashier part of town.

MUM: (*Still looking out the window. She's caught and pulls back. She then waves to the neighbour.*) Shane! I think he's seen me, love. It's islanders. Just like the Indians but fatter nose and lips, love. But they've seen me.

SHANE: You get that when you paste your eyes on the window, Ma.

The phone rings ...

MUM: Shane, don't answer it! Don't answer it! Hello? Hello love, how are you?

Aside.

It's Charlene, love.

SHANE *motions to* MUM *that he isn't home.*

MUM: Sorry, love, Shane's not home right now. Oh, of course you weren't ringing for him, you were ringing for me. It's so lovely of you to still ring and keep in contact with me. If only Shane knew how much of a lovely girl you are, aye.

Aside.

Off you go, it's for me. Go introduce yourself to the new neighbours, suss them out; see what game they're playing. Go on, love! (*back on phone*) Oh, no Shane's not here, I was just thinking to myself, love. How are you anyway?

SHANE: (*Butches up to go meet the neighbour. He opens door and goes over. To TALE*) Hey ... how's it hanging? Thought I'd introduce myself, Shane's the name. I apologise about my mum. Joyce is her name, she keeps to herself pretty much, so I wouldn't get any ideas about friendly introductions, she'd probably call the police. Mum's had a bad run-in with the neighbours before you so she's a bit suspicious, especially when there's new neighbours, we go through them like anything. It's the nature of the beast when you live in a street of state housing. But I don't mind it, aye. It's a quiet street mate, so expect the noise control if you're planning on a party.

TALE: No, no. We are quiet over here, just me and Pina my daughter. My name is Tale. I am from Niue. Small atoll in the South Pacific, not far from Tonga. Only eight hundred and ninety-nine dollars to get there if you lucky to get a special deal. Yeah. We move here from you know GI? Glen Innes, dey call it the eastside, close to da southside opposite da northside but I want to move to the westside. I reckon da bebole here are a good one. See, you did caming over to greet da new neighbours, that's a good sign.

Pause.

SHANE: Cool, cool. So was that your daughter, the girl we saw?

TALE: Yeah, she's a good one. She's studying at university at the moment. This will be her last year. She study political science. I'll send her over with a cake for your mum, she's a good cook Shane. Oh, here. Here she's caming.

PINA: Don't think we didn't see you staring out the window. What! Haven't you seen islanders before? Or are you on neighbourhood watch duty?

SHANE: Calm down, I just came over to say hello, just keeping the peace, sister.

PINA: I'm not your sister! Do I look like your sister? Have I even met you before? No, no, no. Paranoid honky.

SHANE: Sorry, did you just call me a honky, you tight little coconut.

PINA: Oh, you're so funny, NOT! Watch out, Dad, they probably think we're scoping their pad. As if! We'd appreciate it very much if you and the woman didn't stare. It's not polite. I'll get the rest of the stuff, Dad.

TALE: Sorry. You know that daughter of mine is a funny one sometimes, Shane. She always be getting into trouble with her mouth. Not in a bad way, Mr! But in a brainy way. She thinks she knows everything under the sun and how to make the moon. Don't worry about her, I think she gotta woman's problem this week. You know the woman's problem?

SHANE: (*nodding his head*) Yeah, I know where you're angling at, mate. I had a ex-girlfriend that had her period the whole time I was with her. Crazy beasts, women. Look Tale, good to meet you. I hope your daughter finds it in her heart to bake the cake.

TALE: She's a good island girl, Shane. And a brainy one too. You got a girlfriend? She's a single one. I worry sometimes she might be lady-to-lady, you know lady-to-lady? ... It be good to meet you. Say hello to your mother.

SCENE FOUR

Lights at SHANE's house.

SHANE: Ma, the guy's name is Tale, from Niue. Decent guy but very shy, not someone you could go and meet right out. Blokes' kind of man. But he did say he'd send his daughter over with a cake to say hello.

MUM: Laced with arsenic! So you've made best friends with the coconuts next door, have ya! Why don't you just give him the key to the house, Shane, Gawd, whose side are you on?

Phone rings.

MUM: Well, get it!

BRAD is on the phone.

BRAD: Shane, bro. Brad mister in the hiester! Hooked up some major shit for the night, holmes. Pimp on K'Rd reckons he can hook us up the big one balar ... So, looks like the force is strong tonight, balar. What da dilli with that chilli, holmes? Are you up on that shit or what? Here's the deal squeal. The southsider bros are going to be in the Coco and Cabana's crib, so you gotta warm that shit up for the westside, holmes! Check? Check. See you in a couple.

SHANE: The sooner the better, bro. And don't come in. You know the deal, just beep it aye, Ma's on it tonight. Don't approach the house. Sweet? Sweet. (*He hangs up.*)

MUM: You know that boy's a queer, love. I've never known him to have a girlfriend as long as you've known him and that's a bloody long time. He talks funny and he never comes in anymore to give your ma a decent hello. Young man like that being afraid of your ma after a few gins. Ridiculous!

SHANE: Ma, you nearly suffocate the guy every time he's over. He's twenty-two not two. It's all good in the hood, Ma. He'll be here any minute. Don't lay any of yo hassles on him aye.

MUM: Shane! I'm not sure about staying on my own tonight, love. It's just the new neighbours and all and you know how scary I get after a few gins. Stay home with your mum, will ya. Just tonight, love. That man saw me today, love. He'll know I'm on my own if you walk out that door, I'm telling you Shane, I have a bad feeling about that guy. I really do ...

SCENE FIVE

PINA walks up to the door with a cake and knocks.

PINA: Hi. Shane? Hi, just wanted to say sorry about earlier and here's the cake my Dad promised your mum. I didn't bake it, it's bought.

SHANE: Oh, you shouldn't have. Thanks man, I mean girl, I mean ... what you doing tonight? Just wondering perhaps if you wanted to come down to a club that I might be performing at. It's just off Queen St. Coco and Cabana's.

SHANE gives PINA a sexy look.

PINA: Umm, so you're a performer. That's great. Umm no, I've got a huge assignment due and we've just moved in so I don't think it would be a good idea, but thanks for the offer.

SHANE: Are you sure? My mate Brad is swinging by soon and he's got some major shit hooked up, if you know what I mean. There's heaps of room in the car. Front and back.

SHANE gives PINA another sexy look.

PINA: Nah, I better stay in with my dad tonight. That's a great desperate look, man. Maybe some other time when I can put a grass skirt on and let you chase me down the street.

SHANE: I was just looking at you! Relax. What's your problem?

PINA: Oh, so now I've got a problem because you're looking at me like I'm some easy ho.

SHANE: Seriously, I was just looking at you, I didn't mean anything by it.

PINA hands him the cake and leaves.

So does that mean I'll see you there babe? (*He yells out.*) I'll see you there. Yeap. See you there. Here's your cake, Ma.

MUM: I'm not touching that thing, Shane. Who knows what's in it and don't think I didn't see you using the Johnson charm to win that girl over. Charlene's a nice girl, love. Island girls tend to put the beef on in their mature years.

SHANE: Mannnnnn...

He takes a deep breath and looks into the mirror.

How many times can you tell a woman to relax? It's all good. It's all good. I think you just won a heart there, styler. I saw you looking at me. How can you resist the force, baby? The force? The ability to have as much power in your middle finger ...

He points out his middle finger.

... as your tongue.

He flickers his tongue then vigorously wiggles his middle finger.

Five minutes a day never let me down. Anything over and beyond the force ...

He cups his balls.

is God. Pure and simple ...

He raps in front of the mirror.

Pure and simple. Casanova? Obvious. One look? Is all it takes. Twice? And she didn't want you 'cause she never knew you. Three times? Leave the bar and move to a trashier part of town.

The chicks are cheap, then easier to impress. A guy like me can't go wrong in a place like this. It's not too bad down here. Chicky babes! Always more than one, they travel in packs. Thin. Real thin. Hair? Straight, real straight. Legs? Tall, jail-bar thin. Trousers? White, skin-eating tight. Top? Almost less. G-string? Lost to the abyss ...

MUM: Shane, I think Brad's here love. Shall I go outside and invite him in?

SHANE: No, Ma. I've gotta go, we've got stuff to do before we head out and we're rushed already. Easy on the gin and stay inside, Ma. And leave the neighbours alone, OK. I'll see you in the morning. And try to lock up before you go to bed.

MUM: Gawd, Shane, I'm not that worse for wear, am I? I could put something on and show you how the over forties do it. Life begins at forty you know, love. Olivia left Matt by then, I'm sure of it.

SHANE: No, Ma. You always do this when I've got a big night. Just chill out. OK? Gotta go, see you in the morning. I'll catch you up.

SHANE leaves. He sees TALE and waves.

Hey, mate. Look, I hope you don't mind and it's out of full respect that I'm telling you, but I've asked Pina out tonight. I'm performing at a club in town. If she comes, I'll make sure she gets back safe.

TALE: You're a bloody nice guy, mate. Pina tole me you were a performer in the city. You must be a bloody famous, aye. She's not one for going out, but I'll see what I can do. You have a good night anyway, Shane. Thank you for your honest self. See you.

TALE waves him goodbye as they drive off. He then notices MUM and waves to her.

Hello! I'm Tale, new neighbour. I'm not a bad man. Good man. I hope you like the cake.

TALE goes in his house and calls out to PINA.

Pina. Pina! Why are you mean today to Shane? The nice Palagi boy from next door. He's a nice young one too. If you can only look to some of the Palagi boys. He ask me if you like to go to see his performing tonight. You should go. Pina, you know it's a white man's world out there. You'd be wise to find yourself a rich Palagi boyfriend. I'm not stupid, Pina. I see how all those rich Palagis live on the TV. The mothers don't even have to look after the kids because they buy a nana. Can you believe that, Pina? You can buy your own nana ... Here's twenty dollars. Go buy yourself something and go see Shane. I'm going to see if that woman next door is all right, she still standing outside waving. Eh, don't worry about me, just worry to yourself. Stupid!

SCENE SIX

MUM is suggestively waving to TALE.

MUM: Hello. Just wondering if you'd like to join me for a drink. Come on over.

She readjusts furniture and brings TALE in.

Here, take a seat. Thanks ever so much for the cake, haven't had the chance to taste it but it looks real good. Just a bit bored, you know. Kids going out and all, you wonder how you get through sometimes when they get all independent and just dump ya. I've got some gin if you want a nightcap ... not to worry I won't bite.

MUM offers TALE a drink. BRAD sits in the car with SHANE. They drive off.

BRAD: There's a joint in the glove box, spark up bro. Sweet balar.

He has a drink, then a toke on the joint, then hands it back to SHANE.

See that, all good in the hood; your ma's sweet bro.

BRAD hands back beer then turns and swerves.

Just gonna check out the queens on the street before we head into town bro. All good in the hood. Old bloody Edinburgh Street, aye bro.

The car slows down.

Bro, check that shit out, is that a chick or a chick with a dick balar. Here, watch this.

He winds his window down.

What's cooking tonight, biatch?

QUEEN: (*bending over and looking into the car*) Well looks like you boys know how to party, what have you got cooking in there. Looks all good to me, honey. Wanna take us for a ride, babes? Got a head special tonight, two for the price of one, sugar.

BRAD sits back in car. He looks over to SHANE.

BRAD: What you reckon bro? A bit of the tease before we hit the night or what, balar?

He looks at SHANE, no response.

Sorry sistra, we're just cruising tonight. Maybe some other time.

Quick move to outside of the vehicle.

QUEEN: Well, what the fuck you come here for then? Just for a perve I bet. Ladies! We've got some white-trash traders trading.

BRAD: (*Hops back into car and speeds off. Yelling out, looking back.*) Homos!

He looks forward and there's a red light, he slams on the brakes.

Fuck! Red light!

He looks back.

Bro! They're running up the street! Shit, I'm gonna park. I can't move, can't you see the traffic! Hurry before they take their heels off bro.

He quickly parallel parks, alarms his car and begins running

Run bro, run. It's a gay bash, bro!

QUEEN: We're gonna kill you when we catch you! Fucken wankers! We've got rights you know! It's legal in this country now!

SHANE: (*Running on the spot, makes a few turns, looking back once and slowing down*) What the hell was that about bro?! Don't you ever learn your lesson? Shit, they could've taken us out like that, man. Think about it. They're chicks with dicks. Shit bro. I'm getting a cab, man.

He hails.

Taxi! Taxi! Get in bro.

SHANE and BRAD get into the taxi.

DIPTANSHU: I'm not available for the short rides sorry. If I knew you were only going to Queen Street I would not have picked you up. It's busy down there, it will take us at least fifty-five minutes to get from K Road to Queen Street. Please be removing yourselves from my cab. Hold on, wait a minute.

He turns around to see SHANE.

Is that you Shane? Shane Johnson? It's me, Diptanshu. Don't worry about what I just said. I'll take you the quick route. Look I'm terribly, very sorry about the trouble that happened last week. I didn't mean anything by it, if you know what I mean. How is your mother anyway? Tell her I did not mean any disrespect, please tell her that. So I suppose your new neighbours moved in, heard on the dispatch just before you hailed me down. Some island girl giving my last address. Shane, watch out for your mother, she is a terribly, very fragile woman. You must take care of her. Here we go, right outside Coco and Cabana's, the friendly nightspot for those who like to dance their arses off and guys who like to watch. That will be twenty dollars and fifteen cents please. Just make it twenty. Don't look so surprised, I too have a heart. Chin up and you'll have a good night, Shane.

They get out of the taxi.

BRAD: Ah forget Diptanshu, it's fucken Auckland. You'd bump into your own arse if it wasn't behind you. Now, are you set for tonight or what balar? It's a big gig, might just get your lucky break tonight balar. Southside is gonna be representing so you gotta give it up for the westside, balar. Big time. Check? Oh shit, there's the bros man.

They walk up to the bros and shake hands.

Bro! Bro man, it the bros, bro.

He shakes the various hands.

Malo bro, Talofa bro, Kia orana bro, fakaafe atu to you bro ...

Aside.

Fuck I can never get that Niue one down.

Faka faka atu ...

Oh shit. Respect! Respect, Nesian brothers in the house. My boys in town tonight. Catch you up. Fa bros, fa.

To SHANE.

That's respect nigger! Here ...

Hands him drugs.

... take this, scored hot off the westside kitchens. Good source balar. It's in the connections. I'll meet you in the lads'. Peace out!

BRAD and SHANE enter the club and music is pumping with disco lights. SHANE has a look around then enters the toilet where music and lights are dull.

SHANE: Sweet. Sweet, sweet, sweet. Right! Organise yourself, Shane the Shark man. Find empty cubicle. Find hard flat surface. Wipe residue. Pull out bag. Looks to be a nice little gram of the speed there. Check the bag, tap the bag, open the bag, tip the bag, not too much. This shit's sticky. Reach to the left with your left. Fuck, no card! Right pocket, left pocket, back pockets, top pockets. It's a Māori haka mission mate. Check, right top pocket. Relief, community services card and key to the house. Scoop the bag using the key, line up on hard surface, cut and chop, fuck it's sticky. Lick the edge of the card, put in pocket. Roll my fiver and snort that shit up one, up two and the final wipe on the gums. Fuck it, I'll have a bump too. Key in bag. Bump it! Sweet. Fuck that's sore.

BRAD is banging on the toilet door.

BRAD: Bro! Bro man! Are you there? Fuck, have you taken it yet? Oh shit balar! It's the wrong stuff. It's the P bro, it's the pure, you got to smoke that shit, holmes. Ho bro, don't know the effects of that shit straight up your nose.

SHANE: Smoke it. Smoke it! Why didn't you tell me that before man! I'll never be able to perform now. Get inside the club!

A juicy rap beat begins to play.

VOICE ASIDE: Lets give it up to Shane styler westsider!

SHANE: Fuck, they're calling me up for my spot!

BRAD: Then go bro, go!

Rap music plays as lights change back into nightclub.

Shane grabs the microphone to perform his rap.

SHANE: Chicks. Short ones. Tall ones. Skinny ones. Fat ones. Different coloured ones. Chicks. I love it, I won't lie. I could bury myself in one for a week and not come up for air. That's what I'm talking about. The smell. The attitude. Ripe for the plucking, plump for the squeeze, ready for the hunt, can't wait to smell that cunt. Clothes? Suave ones, tight ones, cool ones. I'm vain. I look too long, too hard. Image? Is everything. Thirst means vodka. Labels, give me labels I dig them. Shoes? The first thing a chick checks for after she's decided you're cute. Her labels, your labels thrown across the room left in small piles after the passion of the force. The force? The ability to have as much power in your middle finger as your tongue. Five minutes a day never let me down. Anything over and beyond the force. Is God. Numbers? Don't come in to the equation. Sex machine? It's a curse. Size? Matters, that's why I care. Nine inches cut, baby ...

He retires and takes a bow.

BRAD: That was the shit, balar! The junk star boy! The junk star imposition! Westside to the southside! That's the junk star! Bro man! How's yo blow? Yo blow bro? (*He taps his nose.*) Sweet. Hey, I spotted some fine-ass chocolate honey babe checking you out big time. She's over there hiding in the corner. Look, see, you can hardly see her, but if you squint, it's all good in the hood. Oh shit, Charlene bro ...

CHARLENE enters.

CHARLENE: Brad told me I'd find you down here speeding off your tits. Good set by the way. Bye Brad. Fuck Shane, I don't know how you can hang out with that dumb cunt wigger. He's as black as my arse. I'm surprised he hasn't gotten a good hiding, head kicked in and all. What possesses a white guy to act all black I will never know. It's embarrassing, everyone knows black guys have bigger cocks. You can't pretend that kind of shit, Shane. How are you anyway? Are you seeing anyone?

SHANE: Sorry Char, I can't do this right now, Brad just wrecked me with some P and I can hardly move my jaw.

CHARLENE: Poor babes. Doesn't answer my question though. Are you seeing anybody? You can tell me Shane. I'm over us, I am. I've moved up and Adam. Only rang today to see how your mum was. Really.

SHANE: Well ... yeah I kind of am. I've just only met her so it's early days yet. Nothing serious, just getting to know her. But I told her I'd meet her down here so I better make a move. Good to see you Char.

SHANE moves away and makes his way around the club looking for PINA. He sees her and sneaks up on her.

Boo! My mate Brad said there was a hot chocolate chick checking me out.

PINA: Right about the hot chick, but I was just watching you like everyone else. I saw you talking to my dad. He wouldn't let me stay home. Did you tell him you were a famous star or something ... Oh well ... your mother kind-of asked him over. I told him not to go but you know parents. You can hardly tell them what to do right?

SHANE: Right ... Your dad doesn't drink, does he?

PINA: No! Umm yes. Depends how he's feeling. He'd be too tired to drink tonight with the move and all. Why, is your mum a drinker?

SHANE: No, not really. She does have a few but nothing too heavy. She's not a people person that's for sure. She doesn't like men. She gets into trouble with—

PINA: She invited my dad over. She's not going to freak out on him is she?

SHANE: No! Nothing like that just ... Let's just go for a dance, can't have the best-looking island girl just walk away without a spin on the floor. Come on.

SHANE leads PINA to the dance floor. They begin to dance.

Oh shit! Watch out for my mate Brad. He's a bit wasted.

BRAD: Shit balar! This was the chick I was talking about. She's hot holmes.

To PINA.

Yo hot sister!

Aside to SHANE.

Here, I'll suss her moves out balar. Brad-styler way.

BRAD begins to dance with PINA as the music gets louder. He pumps and grinds her. He goes down on his knees and is hit in the face by her arse. He falls back, the music stops as he looks around with embarrassment. The music starts again and he quickly gets up.

To the lads', bro. Now.

To PINA.

Sorry babes, I'll bring him back. If that's what you want.

Gives her a sexy look.

Just playing, sister.

He walks quickly into the toilet. Toilet lights.

Fuck man, what the dilli with dat shit holmes. That pussy came screaming from nowhere balar. Whoa! Cunt surprise, brother! Right there. (*touches his lips*) In with a grin, man. I think she wants me. Too hot to trot. Tu meke to da daze bro. Life is like a box of chocolate, balar. Don't know what you're going to get till you eat it out balar ...

He unzips and proceeds to piss in urinal.

Shh! Hear that? Shh. Fucken homos bro, listen to them ...

Makes light butch sex sounds then starts to wank himself while standing at the urinal.

Oh fuck, I hate the homos aye bro. Nah I do, bro. Really. No lies aye bro. I fucken hate them, aye bro.

He's just about to cum.

Homos, homos ... hate them bro, bro, bro, bro. Oh fuck! Brauuuuuuuugh!

Just playing bro. Relax. Serious, serious. Chill out balar.

SHANE: Yeah bro. Hilarious. What you think about Pina, man. She's different from the other girls I've had. There's something about that one. I told her dad I'd bring her home if we hooked up. I mean bro, what's that about.

BRAD: You mean that's the same chick that's just moved in next door. Bro! Are you crazy! She's probably got five brothers waiting outside. And uncles and cousins. They'll kill you, man. Don't think I haven't looked at those girls before bro, I have, but it's all big trouble in little island if you connect. It's machete central balar!

Come on now. How long have we known each other bro? I wouldn't put you wrong bro. What would your ma say bro?

Lights change to SHANE's house.

MUM: You know Tale. You're awfully kind and sweet. Thanks for drinking with me. I got myself all flustered. Don't you miss her now that she's getting older? Your daughter? I miss Shane when he's at work and out all the time. You know, it feels as if I've known you for ages. It really does. I'm not just saying that ... Do you mind if I have another one? Gawd, that's much better. I don't usually drink this much. Not with strangers anyway, but you can hardly call us strangers. We're practically... well, I don't know what. Feels like the kids have brought us together. Do you mind if I have another one?

Lights back to nightclub toilets.

SHANE: Bro, it's just her and her pops. I met him today. He's having drinks with Ma. It's sweet bro, I know what I'm doing. And let's not fret about the island bros I'm down with the kung fu styles. (*He does a few quick kung fu moves.*) Shit, that P's alight!

Lights change back to SHANE's house where MUM and TALE are having drinks. TALE is sitting down addressing MUM as she stands over him.

TALE: Joyce. You are the most honest, beautiful lady I have met in a very long time. Your son has your eyes. Like stars. Twinkle, twinkle. You know?

Lights change back to club and PINA is waiting for SHANE.

PINA: Finally. I was just about to leave. What were you guys doing in there? Forget I asked that. You've got shit all dripping out of your nose Shane.

BRAD: Oh sister. It's my fault. I scored the P thinking it was speed. Shane's the good type. A real loyal to the daze type. He's not into P, are you bro? Bro ...

PINA: Sorry about the dance floor. Hope you didn't hurt yourself. So, you guys been on the P. You know that stuff is shit. You didn't strike me as the type of guy that would be into plastic, Shane.

PINA is pushed by CHARLENE as she come through looking for SHANE.

CHARLENE: (*to PINA*) Sorry hon, have you got any clean ashtrays? Oh sorry, you must be Shane's new project. Charlene Hanson. It's so easy to find the boys. Always standing outside the little boys' room. How's it going Bradster wigger.

To SHANE.

Can I talk to you for a sec?

Indiscreetly to SHANE.

Hi I hope you didn't think I was being racist. It just isn't cool to be racist these days. Anyways I love black people. My God! Big ups to J Lo and D-Child. Big ups! See Shane, I'm not racist. I just want ... I really think things will work out if you give it a chance babes. I just need to know what you want from me. What's your problem anyway?

Lights change back to SHANE's house where MUM and TALE are having drinks. TALE is sitting down; MUM stands over him.

MUM: Do you really think so Tale? No stop it. You're just saying that. You shouldn't tease me. You wouldn't like me when I feel teased ...

Lights change back to nightclub.

SHANE: Charlene it's not a good time right now. I'm taking Pina home, we were just about to leave. Good to see you, we'll catch up sometime. Peace out Brad. Come on Pina, let's go.

BRAD: Bro, you can't leave now. The bros want to have a drink with you. Bro! It's your big break. Balar!

SHANE leaves.

Poofter! Come on, Char, I'll take you for a dance.

CHARLENE: (*dancing unfulfilled*) It's not fair, Brad. What has she got that I don't have? Can't you talk to him?

BRAD: (*dancing*) Sister, you know Shane. He's his own balar. He's not going to listen to what I have to say on the situation. You just gotta shift that shit.

SCENE SEVEN

SHANE is outside the club and hails a taxi

SHANE: Taxi! Taxi!

Sweet. You can stop laughing now. I can see you're laughing on the inside. Get into the cab. Coburg Street Henderson thanks.

PINA sits in cab at the back with SHANE. She shuffles around and is a little uncomfortable.

PINA: So, that's your ex-girlfriend, Charlene Hanson I take it. And your best friend Brad. Interesting ... I'm everyone's sister tonight ... So why did you break up with her?

SHANE: (*peaking off his P hit*) Didn't want to wake up next to some chick with two babies in the bed and another two on a mattress on the floor, still stuck at my mother's house staring at the ceiling wondering how the fuck did I get here. Charlene got pregnant twice in the six months we went out and she kept saying she took the pill. Two abortions later and she starting talking to my mother about kids and how great it would be. 'Great, great, great ... ' Dead end street, that one. I seem to attract the ones who get pregnant on the pill. Not that you're one of those kind of girls, Pina.

PINA: Woeeee P-head. One sentence at a time. Nah, just playing. You should tell her that sometime, I think she needs to hear it.

SHANE: That's a very clever thing to say, Pina. Thanks. So ... your dad's hooking it up with my ma aye?

PINA: No! No, absolutely not. He has been popular with the ladies but he's over that now. My mum left him 'cause he couldn't keep it in his pants. She left me to look after him. It's strange when parents break up. They leave the kid as well as their other half. Well, that's what happened with me. Haven't seen my mother for years. How about your dad?

SHANE: Ah! I've heard my mum calling out this name in her sleep. I think that's him. I've been curious but I reckon it's best to let dead dogs lie after a while. I'm not like you. Don't have my life planned ahead of me at all aye. Probably be living in the same house for the rest of my life.

PINA: It's the drugs talking, Shane. It's just a degree I'm finishing, doesn't mean I'll get a job. Anyway, you don't have to know what you want. Why should you? I think people place too much responsibility on people our age. We should just learn about what life has to offer and worry about the other stuff later. Right? I think that's why women in their thirties probably have better sex. They've figured out all men are the same and have stopped trying to work them out. So they enjoy it more. That's what I read in *New Woman* ... Look our street. Number 22, thanks driver. Don't worry, I'll pay for the cab, it's the least I can do.

To taxi driver.

You're kidding! Fifty bucks! I've got it.

She gives taxi driver the money.

Thanks driver.

DIPTANSHU: (*turning to SHANE*) Thank you very much. You have a good morning, Shane.

SHANE: (*to PINA*) Long story. Come over to mine for a bit. Let's sit down and talk some more, I don't think I'll be able to kip until next week. This P's got me wired. We can sit outside. I won't get violent, I don't even like the stuff ... Come on, I wouldn't try to get you in the sack. Hey, you just moved in. Save that trick for next weekend ... Nah, just playing. Come on. I'm not going to bite. If you don't want me to ... Just playing! We'll sit on the front door step.

PINA: Yeah all right! You know my dad only likes you because you're a Palagi. He's always wanted me to marry a Palagi, thinks I'd have a better life. ''Cause the world we live in is a white man's world, Pina. White men, white women, black men, then last of the heap, black women.' So he figures if I latch onto a Palagi I'll be better placed in the scheme of things.

SHANE: Funny you should mention that. I agree with him. Fully. And furthermore, I am one.

PINA: Funnily enough I don't agree with my father. Funny aye ...

SHANE: Wow ... You can think for yourself, too ...

PINA: Funny. Not! Who the ... Nah, just playing. See, I can play too ...

SHANE: You're a bit of a babe.

PINA: You're a bit of a babe.

SHANE: You're a bit of a babe.

PINA: You're a bit of a babe.

Lights change into dim bedroom where TALE and MUM are rooting.

MUM: You've got the spirit of the dingo in ya. You have, Tale.

Lights change back to SHANE and PINA on his front doorstep.

SHANE: If you could see how beautiful I think you are ... You'd never stop licking yourself ... your face, your arms, your legs, your fingers, can I suck one of your fingers?

PINA: Piss off, you're wasted. You're funny. You're a sweet guy Shane, but. Nah. It's not that I don't want to, it's just ... I've got all this shit I have to do and there's no room for boyfriends. You'll only sweep me off my feet and make me so lovesick I'd be vomiting every day. A boyfriend that lives next door as well? There's no way ...

She leans in to kiss him.

BRAD: Is that you bro? Sorry for the interruption. Shit, aren't you guys cold out here? (*to SHANE*) Can I see you for a sec bro? Bro, don't you think there's something we need to yarn about? I'm not down with you just taking off that way, aye bro. I just got back from looking everywhere for you man. My fucken car's been smashed up too. What the dilli with that shit holmes. I had to borrow Charlene's wheels bro and listen to her shit. I just had enough time to leave her down the road at the gas station. She's spending my last ten bucks on mince and cheese pies bro. What the dilli, you take my fucken drugs and piss off on me. I'm not no nigger you can spit on and kick down when you're feeling all insecure. Is this about those homos in the toilet?

Enter CHARLENE.

CHARLENE: I knew it! You're homos. I knew you'd walk here Brad, so I followed you. I should have known all along. Boys' toilet. You two always take the longest time. There was no way you dropped me for nothing, Shane. Ha! Finally an answer! You're homos! Dirty homos!

Enter TALE.

TALE: What the hell is going on here? Who's being a homo? Hey, I saw you before. You the guy who was beeping his horn today. You Shane's friend.

He sees PINA.

Pina! What are you doing here?

PINA: What are you doing here, Dad! You have got to be joking!

TALE: Are these boys homos?

To SHANE and BRAD

Why, you dirty homos! You trying to be homo with my daughter, aye!

Enter MUM.

MUM: Shane's not a homo, he's a stud with the ladies, aren't you, love.

TALE: Pina, you better get your black bum inside the house before I kill it!

BRAD: Yo, yo, yo let's just chill out here everyone, it's been a long night, I'm sure we could all do with a bit of the old shut-eye.

MUM: What's all the fuss? Tale, calm down, love. It's just the kids getting to know each other.

CHARLENE: So you're not a homo? Then why in the hell are we broken up!

SHANE: Would you shut up, Charlene, and go home.

MUM: Well, Shane Michael Johnson you should be ashamed of yourself. In all my life. Get here ...

She talks to SHANE aside.

You're really ruining it for me, love. I've found a real connection with this one, why do you have to spoil it for me?

PINA: I can't believe you'd do this, Dad. I can't believe you couldn't just keep your pants on for one night. You're so embarrassing!

TALE: Hey, young lady! You watch your mouth! I'm your father, not your mate!

MUM: Come on, Tale, come back to bed, love.

PINA: You slut! You fucken whore! How dare you tell my father what to do!

TALE: Hey you shut up!

PINA: Fine! I'm out of here. Keep your whore!

TALE: Don't you walk away when I'm talking to you, young lady.

SHANE: Pina! I'm sorry ... Why, Ma! I told you to stay inside.

TALE: Hey! You leave her alone.

SHANE: Bro, don't tell me how to talk to my ma all right, you're a dime a fucken dozen.

TALE: Hey! That was my daughter, you bastard!

SHANE: Yeah! And that's my mother, you cunt!

They fist-fight. TALE smashes SHANE.

MUM: Shane! Shane, love! Are you all right? Someone call an ambulance! I don't think he's breathing. Help! Help!

Blackout.

SCENE EIGHT

Lights crossfade into a hospital.

MUM: Love, it's me, your mother. You're at the hospital. Oh you're with us, thank gawd. Well, a fine mess you got yourself into this morning. Fuck's sake, love. Doctor said shouldn't be long. (*pause*) You've got ... you've got concussion. They're not too sure about how bad, still waiting on tests. I popped home to pick you up a few things. Pina's left you a note at the door. She's gone. Left. Moved out, love. I saw her, she was very upset when she was leaving, had all her bags packed. Left Tale crying at the gate when she jumped in the cab. I'm sorry, love ... Charlene's a lovely looking girl, could have a good yarn with that one ... I know I'm to blame, love ... It's, it's not easy being me ... I try ... It's our home and Tale can bloody well move out if he's got a problem. Not much point having a two bedroom when there's only one in the house. You know I love ya, don't ya love.

Lights fade back to factory.

SCENE NINE

SHANE continues his story amid the factory hum. He stacks boxes and is lost for words at first.

SHANE: That's right! It's two hundred and twenty-four thousand bubbles in a twelve-metre roll of bubble wrap. I can't remember ... What was I talking about? ... The depression ... the pot ... A few bubbles popped ... dent in the protection ... Pina ... She'd left her dad and she left me that morning. Over the week I've been sleeping, dreaming about her ... Tale reckons I'm to blame. Mum told me it's not my fault ... but I'll keep looking ... Doubles. Quiet. No one round. Just me, the shit and the boxes ... Gives me a chance to think, make shit up in my head. Wake up and smell the plastic ...

Blackout.

NEW ZEALAND PLAY SERIES PRESENTS

FALEMALAMA
FROM SAMOA TO NIUE TO NEW ZEALAND AND BACK AGAIN

INTRODUCTION

I knew before I wrote my first professional piece for the stage, *Mapaki*, that I would one day interpret and write my mother's stories.

I lived next door to my mother from 1995 to 2000. In those years I heard many stories of her life. I grew to know her as a friend, enemy, bank, babysitter and mum. I didn't move very far from her when I did finally move out of the unit next door, and she still had more stories to share as she continued her role as housecleaner and gardener in my new three-bedroom home down the road. I was at university; I think it was her way of supporting me on my journey with my two young children. Although, when times got skint, she would nag me about getting a job at the chicken factory in West Auckland. She didn't see the point of all this time away from my kids with no money to show for it. She did when she attended my graduations, though, she was as proud as an 'island woman' could be. That's hard-out pride, hard.

Pangea World Theater, a small theatre company based in Minneapolis, commissioned me to write *Falemalama*. They were celebrating their 10th Indigenous Voices Series. I first met the Literary Manager of the company, Meena Natarajan, in Athens, where she invited me to perform *Mapaki* in 2001. This is where I met the Artistic Director of the company, Dipankar Mukherjee, who was greatly inspired by my work and style. We got on famously with our debates on fascism, poverty, and being immigrants of colour in America. Dipankar and Meena opened the door to the American indigenous theatre market for me at that time.

In 2006 Meena heard I was in Canada, acting in a theatre show that was touring for five weeks. She contacted me about a commission, a new work that I could start immediately if I was up to it. It didn't take me long to make up my mind and I was writing in the second week of being in Canada. Once the tour wound up in Vancouver my sister Fe'eta, who lives in Seattle, came and picked me up. I hibernated in her house for one month and continued to resurrect the memory of my mother in full force in the billowing cold Seattle winter. I wrote *Falemalama*, learnt the piece, then made a show with my pregnant niece Bianca in my sister's rumpus room, ready for an opening night of 200 strangers across country in Minneapolis. It was a preview, so no critics, but beautiful letters and emails from audience members who got it...

> I guess what I'm trying to say is that your mother's story became my mother's story ... in a way. Yes, there are numerous differences, and those differences are significant. But I think it is the commonalities that allowed me to connect so intimately with your piece, that led me to cry repeatedly even hours after your show ended. But I must say that even if my Omma's story did not overlap with your mother's story, I would still have been affected just as powerfully because at the end of your performance, I cared for Falemalama. I cared about her well-being, her dreams, her desires. I wanted her to succeed, to reunite with Michael, with Ikinofo.
>
> Soojin Pate (Minneapolis, 20 November 2006)

I knew how much I would miss my mother when it was her time to go. I knew I'd miss her immensely. All the things that used to annoy me about her are now non-existent. One day her singing voice outside my window weeding, next day no singing. Ignoring the morning phone calls that rang with her name on it, to no 7am calls anymore. Running away from her weirdness, to no weirdness like hers in my life again. No Mum, no more.

Dianna Fuemana
Auckland 2008

Original Production

First performed at the Pangea World Theater, Minneapolis
16 November 2006

with the following cast and creative team:

All characters played by Dianna Fuemana

Directing by Dipankar Mukherjee

Rehearsal directing by Bianca Tolua

Choreography/Sāmoan Transliteration by Sasamamao Siatu'u

Advisor: Fe'eta Fuemana-Cruz

Original soundtrack by Igelese Ete

Characters

STORYTELLER: Narrator.

TIEN (short for THEEND): Sāmoan woman in her thirties. This is her story, her recollection of her mother's life.

FALEMALAMA (FALE shortened): Sāmoan woman whose first language is Sāmoan. Ages from teenager to elderly woman.

MOTHER: Falemalama's mother.

LINDA: Fa'afāfine[1] in her twenties living in Pago Pago. Falemalama's best friend.

TANIELA: Falemalama's Niue husband.

NANA: Taniela's mother. Lives in Niue.

LUIATA: Falemalama's sister-in-law.

TONGA: Taniela's brother.

---

[1] A male who is raised, dresses and behaves as a woman – a traditional part of society in Sāmoa and other parts of the Pacific, often in families where there are too many boys.

Settings

Tien's kitchen – Tien is aged in her late 20s. Fale is aged late 50s. Present day.

Dream time Amerika Sāmoa – A warm memory set in Pago Pago.

Dream time Niue – A cold memory set in the village of Mutalau.

Dream time New Zealand – Set in New Zealand 1970s–80s.

Projection

A 'family portrait' projection of Fale in Amerika Sāmoa in the 60s with her four young children seated amongst the bush on a finely woven mat.

Author's notes

The story is set in Amerika Sāmoa, Niue and New Zealand, spanning a period of 64 years.

Any number of actors can play out this story.
The original production was performed by a sole actress.
The second production involved one actress and one actor.
The interpretation is left open to the director.
Musician(s) play traditional Sāmoan instruments live to evoke the story.

Music

This poignant story, telling of Falemalama's life journey, is depicted in various Pacific musical elements. The most pivotal are the various traditional Pacific songs, which are sung solo by the storyteller intermittently throughout the play. Songs which are popular with the Sāmoan and Pacific peoples, like 'Lota Nu'u' (My country) and 'Fa'afetai i le Atua' (Thank you God), bring a sense of Pacific pride, patriotism, identity and nostalgia. Simultaneously, it evokes Fale's afflictions, vulnerability and gratitude.

The underlying musical soundscape is based on the traditional Pacific instruments: fala (a rolled mat commonly used in Sāmoa), pātē (log drum) and foafoa (conch). This accompanies the traditional Sāmoan dance movements. The Pacific instrumentation interweaves and fuses with the western orchestral/popular instruments, aiding the creation of sounds and genres stereotypical of the times.

Two instrumentation concepts are used to manifest the mana (inner power) of Falemalama. One is the heartbeat, represented by the various Pacific drums and body percussion; the second is the breath of life, depicted by the solo voice and the foafoa. These musical sounds illustrate and celebrate Falemalama's legacy.

Igelese Ete (Musical Director)

Movement

Traditional and contemporary Sāmoan movement is used throughout the piece. It is up to the choreographer or director as to where these movements are used.

In SCENE FOUR there is a fan dance to be performed, using Sāmoan fans to show the love between the two characters. Niue movements are to be used in the singing of the Niue anthem.

SCENE FIVE has a spear dance that is for Fale who is gathering fish for her family.

In SCENE EIGHT where the story migrates to New Zealand, traditional or contemporary Māori movements, or both, are used to show that journey.

SCENE TEN has a movement-based direction which should encapsulate the lives of 42 direct descendants of Falemalama – her children, grandchildren and great-grandchildren – at the time of her death. This is open to the choreographer/director to interpret through Sāmoan dance. However, there should be 42 set movements in the phase.

A taualunga is the last item to be performed to officially close the story. The taualunga of a taupou is an elegant dance that portrays the beauty, elegance and dignity of the Sāmoan culture.

FALEMALAMA

SCENE ONE

Dream time Amerika Sāmoa.

The story is opened by an introductory/welcoming dance to the sound of drums.

A Sāmoan prayer is recited.

Fa'afetai Tamā mo le ola 'ua e.
'aumaia ia te a'u fa'apea lo'u 'āiga.
Fa'amāgalo a'u agasala ma e ita mai ia te a'u.
Foa'i mai le mālosi pe a ou vaivai.
Fa'amanuia 'oe Tamā le 'ua ālolofa mai ia te a'u.
Lavea'i ia'i mātou ai le leaga ma fa'alatalata o mātou tagata ia te 'oe.
Foa'i mai le mālosi ma.
Fa'asino mai ou ala le suafa.
'O Iesu
'Āmene.[2]

---

[2] Thank you Lord for my life.
Thank you Lord for the life of my family.
Forgive me for my sins and for those who sin against me.
Give me the strength to stand up when I am down.
Bless all of the people I love and who love me.
Keep us safe from harm and bring us closer to you.
Give me strength.
Show me your path.
In Jesus' name
Amen.

The STORYTELLER arrives centre stage. She sings.

STORYTELLER: Oh, I never will forget you.

Sāmoa e nei galo atu.

Oh, I never will forget you.

Sāmoa e nei galo atu ...

TIEN: Her name was Falemalama.

Falemalama.

Falemalama!

Falemalama Abbey Reid. Her mother, American Sāmoan. Father, 'afakasi (half-caste) Sāmoan, Northern European. She was the only kid they had together. Only child to her mother.

Father she never knew, went on to marry other woman and have children littered everywhere. From Sāmoa to New Zealand to Hawai'i to America and God knows where else. He was never there for her. Not when she was young. Not when she was old.

STORYTELLER: She was born in Futiga, Amerika Sāmoa, February 8th, 1942. It was a sweltering afternoon. The hottest day recorded in over 50 years. There was no hospital.

Only a broken down house where her mother

pushed

and

pushed

until Falemalama swooped in her first breath of air amongst the coconut and banana trees waiting outside.

A breath.

TIEN: If only she knew what was coming, she would've crawled back in. But no one knows that. Only God. And, as Falemalama would say, 'Ua na'o le Atua na te iloa mea 'uma.'[3]

---

[3] Only God knows everything.

Her mother married a man who didn't like Fale. Her mother wasn't any different.

Her discontent with her child varied, beating her not only with her hands, but sepelus too.

Sepelus?

STORYTELLER: Big bush knives that are used in civil wars in Africa in lieu of fast shooting guns. In the islands we use them to cut grass, weeds, branches, trees…

SCENE TWO

TIEN's kitchen.

TIEN: I remember coming home with my new number two haircut, trying to liberate myself as a strong, independent woman who didn't care what other people thought. Even if I did look like a lesbian!

FALE knocks on TIEN's door.

FALE: Tien. Tien! Tatala le faitoto'a![4]

Door opens. She pulls off her hat.

TIEN: And there in front of me stood a mirror!

TIEN: Mum! What the hell have you done?

FALE: 'E tutusa lava i taua.[5] I'm a young one, too.

TIEN: Mum! You can't do that.

FALE: Salapu lou gutu.[6]

TIEN: I closed the door on her. I was hell annoyed.

Re-enactment.

FALE: Tien … Tien … Baby, tatala le faitoto'a! Don't be silly, little girl.

TIEN: I opened the door and she came into my kitchen.

---

[4] Open the door!
[5] I'm like you too.
[6] Oh shut your mouth.

FALE: You want a cup of tea?

Why you got a dirty house for?

I come clean and clean.

You never say thank you, never.

TIEN: Just as my eyes went to roll over at her, they stuck focused on the top of her head.

'Mum, how did you get that crack in the middle of your head? It's so big.'

I remembered the thick scar ingrained across her left wrist.

FALE: I told you. My mum smack my hand, smack my head.

Never mind, baby.

'O le Atua na te silafia mea 'uma.[7]

I still love my mum.

STORYTELLER: On her account she left home at 13 and had left school by the time she was 10. Cast into the small island city, she was a street kid, hungry but free.

She'd hung around the local bar where all the men and 'dirty' women would congregate after a long, hot day at the plantations. There were a lot of foreigners.

Men mainly.

Naval officers, trade merchants,

white men looking for exotic Polynesian wives,

white men looking for exotic sex with Polynesian woman.

White men everywhere fucking everything that would open up.

Amerika Sāmoa and Western Sāmoa have German Sāmoans, Northern European Sāmoans, French Sāmoans, Scottish Sāmoans, Irish Sāmoans, Swedish Sāmoans – there is a steep pride in the touch of the white blood that runs in some Sāmoan families.

---

[7] God sees everything.

'Oh, she's so fair ... She's so pretty, look at her nose, it's so straight, oh, she's so slim.'

Thank God for all the white foreigners who copulated in Sāmoa!

Falemalama was one of those children.

The only thing he left her, Mr Hubert Reid, was his last name. Reid.

Not that it ever got her anywhere.

Introducing Falemalama's next chapter of life. A Sāmoan song is sung and dance is performed.

Sāmoana – Sāmoana
Ala mai – Ala mai
Fai ai nei – Fai ai nei
Le faʻafetai – Le faʻafetai
I le pule ia maua i
ʻO lou nuʻu i le vasa.[8]

SCENE THREE

Tien's kitchen.

FALE: Tien. Tien. Tien! What you doing? You sleep, sleep, sleep all time. You silly little girl.

TIEN: At the time, there was nothing worse than waking up to the sound of her voice whining, reminding, screaming until I got up and out of my bed. Always stories, dreams, visions of the future, visions of the past. I'd sip up the coffee, sit and listen.

FALE: Eh! One day I'm going to be dead and you be sorry.

I had a dream about my friend Linda.

---

[8] Sāmoa – Sāmoa
　　Awake – Awake
　　Offer – Offer
　　Great thanks
　　For the authority to remain
　　My country in the ocean.

I use to stay with her when my mum chased me out.

She was very kind to me. She use to go by the pub and be friends with the men.

LINDA waves, then winks.

Thank the Lord she take care of me at that time. I was only a young girl. But when she found out I was pregnant...

LINDA: Se aikae! Mākagā kele lou amio![9]

FALE: And that's when I met your dad. Taniela. My friend told me to go and take his watch to fix it up. I don't know what I am thinking at that time but the man open the door and I stayed with him from that day. It was your dad. When my mum find out what I am doing ...

MOTHER: Se aikae! Mākagā kele lou amio! Kaoga alu i le fale te'i fasioki![10]

STORYTELLER: He told her mother to leave. She was apparently devastated and disowned Falemalama from that day onward. Well, actually, she was one of his ex-girlfriends. Oops. Taniela was 16 years older than Fale.

TIEN: Dad told me the story of how he followed her one morning in Pago Pago, weeks after she had given birth to the illegitimate child. She named him Michael, and one of Taniela's best friends adopted him.

TANIELA: I see Fale walking across into the bushes. I follow her and she walking down past the bush, past the shop, past the hospital and to a small house. She look left: she look right. I can hear a baby crying inside the house. Really crying. She hop inside the window and take Michael out of the cot. The parents left him by himself and tie a bottle to the side to feed him. Fale took him out and give him her titty. She do this a lot. I never tell

---

[9] You little shit! You are shameful!
[10] You little shit! You are shameful! You better get home now before I kill you right here!

her because I don't know what to do.

STORYTELLER: Falemalama fell pregnant again, to Taniela this time, and he asked her to marry him.

Registration office: small, hot, sticky, but quick.

A birth dance is performed for all the children.

FALE: Birth of the first child, at home: a girl, named Malia. Chubby as a cherub, sick with flu.

Panting, pushing ...

Birth of second child: Fia, another girl. Born in the hospital, premature, underweight, sicker than Malia.

Panting, pushing ...

Birth of third child: Suria, another girl. Born by the umu pit[11] just before the food was coming up. Not sick at all.

Panting, pushing ...

Joy to the world. Birth of the fourth child: Tavaki. Finally, a son for Taniela.

Relax.

STORYTELLER: Fale quickly learned how to fofō, a healing massage.

She relied on prayer to help her sick children recover.

Her mother didn't care: as far as she was concerned, Fale got what she deserved.

LINDA giving FALE the TALK.

LINDA: Fale, I've seen Taniela down at the city drinking with other woman. Eh, give the kids to your mother, she doesn't have any and she has a big 'āiga. There are lots of Palagi men in town. You want to go to America? You have a better life there. There's lots money. Don't suffer your life. Give the kids to your family.

---

[11] stone oven

STORYTELLER: Falemalama cried that night to the sound of flapping coconut trees and barking dogs in the still, black night. The tears running off her cheeks flooded the crest between her breasts. Tavaki woke on her lap and she gently placed her nipple in his mouth. He cried, too, a little, when tasting the salty, tear-soaked breast. The girls asleep on the floor all huddled up like puppies.

FALE: (*sings a Sāmoan song*) Lota nu'u na oe fānau ai
'Ua lelei oe i le vasa
'Ua e maua mai lugā
'O le tofi a'ogā.[12]

Song ends.

Taniela, where you been?

The children are hungry.

You promise me you look after me.

You promise to look after the kids.

Why you running away?

You a liar!

STORYTELLER: That next morning, Falemalama's battered voice could be heard screaming from the welts of a hard hand smacking her down.

She kept getting up for more, hoping that one of the hits would knock her out for good. Take away the light and leave her in a blissful darkness. A darkness unknown, but surely better than the light she knew that day. The girls huddled with the baby and cried.

Taniela stopped. But Fale's flame had been ignited. She tore off her clothes with a roar and ran through the village screaming.

The children cried more as the sight of their naked mother fell

---

[12] My country where I was born
You are the best in the entire world
You have obtained authority from above
To rule.

on the eyes of all the other villagers.

'She's crazy, she's a crazy ...'

Taniela ran out and caught her in his arms. Fale was never the same after that day.

SCENE FOUR

Dream time Amerika Sāmoa.

STORYTELLER: Taniela decided the best thing to do was to take his family to his own island. The island of Niue. New life, old family, old friends. It was time to take his family home.

FALE: Before we left, Taniela came home with a camera. I had never had my photo taken before. I bathed the children in the tub outside.

In a small, cracked mirror, which I kept underneath a mat, I checked myself.

I loved him. I loved him a lot ...

TANIELA puts a flower in her ear. A fan dance is performed.

STORYTELLER: The children brought over a fine woven mat. They jumped on with little baby Tavaki being thrown between the three sisters. Giggling and laughing, they were all greased up with coconut oil, hair combed up and out, dresses fluffed.

Taking the family portraits.

TANIELA: Come, kids, go sit next to your mother. Sit down, sit down. Fale, hold Tavaki. OK, everybody ready? Eh, sit down ... taha, ua, tolu.[13]

Blackout. A flash cuts into 'Family Portrait' of Falemalama and kids, which can be seen projected onto the back wall.

TIEN: This was the only photo we had of our family in Amerika Sāmoa. It was 1966, time to board the *Tofua*: the ship of dreams that took families around the Pacific Islands to find their new

---

[13] one, two, three.

destiny. Tavaki was less than a year old, Suria was three, Fia was four and Malia was six.

STORYTELLER: It stung Fale's heart to know she was leaving her first-born son behind. But she had to believe it was for the best. They boarded the *Tofua*, Taniela's hands clasping tightly around her waist and the children hanging onto both parents.

As the ship pulled away, Fale caught a glimpse of her mother standing behind the waving hands of other people. Their eyes locked and Fale waved. She was truly leaving home.

Projection off.

Going to Niue

Niue Anthem:

Ko e Iki he Lagi
Kua fakaalofa mai
Ki Niue nei, ki Niue nei
Kua pule totonu
E Patuiki toatu
Kua pule okooko ki Niue nei

Ki Niue nei
Ki Niue nei
Ki Niue nei
Ki Niue nei

Kua pule oko oko
Ki Niue nei
Kua pule ki Niue nei.[14]

SCENE FIVE

Dream time Niue. The boat arrives in Niue.

STORYTELLER: The Alofi wharf in Niue was packed with people waving, jumping up and down, all excited with the new arrivals. As soon as the ship docked, the children ran down the plank with Taniela following closely.

---

[14] The Lord in Heaven
Who loves Niue
Who rules kindly
The Almighty
Who rules completely over Niue

Over Niue
Over Niue
Over Niue
Over Niue

Who rules completely over Niue
Who rules over Niue.

Fale was surprised to see the island was so small. Not as big as her own.

Five women headed in her direction and were cut off by the children. They picked the children up and smothered them with kisses and hugs. Some were crying and touching Taniela's long-lost face. They were his sisters. He introduced them one by one, and one by one they gave Fale a smile and a quick peck on the cheek.

FALE: It's a real family.

STORYTELLER: They drove for about ten minutes to the village of Mutalau, where Taniela's family were from. Fale noticed the houses were little hurricane huts with cookhouses and drop toilets at the back. But there were no pigs running around, no cows. She wondered what they ate.

There was a formal welcoming. Taniela presented his family with the boxes of biscuits, tins of corned beef and milk powder they had brought over with them.

NANA: Fakaalofa lahi atu ki mutolu oti.[15]

Taniela has been away too long...

It's a shame his children weren't born in Niue...

It was a shame we weren't at your wedding...

We hope you have chosen well and your family will be a strong addition to the existing families and not a burden...

Tulou, tulou mua tulou.[16]

STORYTELLER: That night, as the children settled into their new hut, Taniela went and had a drink with his brothers. It had been eight years since he had seen them. A sister-in-law came to visit. Her name was Luiata.

---

[15] Greetings to you all.
[16] Thank you, thank you, thank you very much.

LUIATA: Fakaalofa lahi atu[17] Fale. Welcome to my husband's family. Taniela was very lucky to live in Amerika Sāmoa. Lucky to marry one too, eh. I thought I better come and tell you a few hints that will make your stay in Niue a little more comfortable ...

Never talk to the mother, only when she talks to you.

Never answer back to the sisters, they will beat you.

Never wear your hair out, they will think you are trying to steal other men.

Never let anyone hear you argue with Taniela, they will beat you.

Never look at his brothers. He has three. Taiula, Tonga and my husband Lui.

Never ask for food, it's up to Taniela to get it for you and the family.

Always smack your children if they do anything the others might think is wrong.

Do this and you will be all right, all right?

FALE: Taniela been away in the bush for three days hunting uga. We are hungry. I take my kids to the reef to catch a fish.

Spear dance.

FALE makes a little spear from the branches in the bush, shaving off a pointy end with her sepelu. She spears three fish. She makes a fire and feeds the children. She is caught by TANIELA.

TANIELA: Fale!

FALE quickly gets up and goes to him.

What the hell are you doing? Didn't Luiata tell you?

FALE: We were hungry.

---

[17] Greetings

TANIELA: I was going to get the food. Why can't you wait like all the other woman in the village?

FALE: You want us to starve?

TANIELA: The women are not allowed to climb coconut trees!

Not allowed to go fishing.

Not allowed to go into the bush by themself.

You know how that looks?

FALE: I took the children!

TANIELA beats FALE. She slowly retreats.

SCENE SIX

Dream time Niue. Two weeks later ...

LUIATA visits a beaten-down FALEMALAMA.

LUIATA: Fale ... Fale, it's Luiata ...

You all right?

I brought you some food.

You been inside for two weeks.

They're telling your children lies about you. You have to go and get them. Don't leave them with the sisters, that's what they want. Don't let them get to you. Fale?

FALE: Three years we stay. We are poor. Poor, poor. I hate this place.

STORYTELLER: Two more new arrivals.

FALE: Birth of fifth child in Niue: a boy, Iosua. Born dark with straight hair.

Birth of sixth child in Niue: another boy, Ikinofo. Born big and bouncy.

STORYTELLER: Fale couldn't help but think about Michael back in Pago Pago, and how he must've grown.

FALE: (*prays*)

> Fa'afetai Tamā mo le ola 'ua e
> 'aumaia ia te a'u faapea lo'u aiga.
> Fa'amāgalo a'u agasala ma 'e ita mai ia te a'u.
> Foa'i mai le mālosi pe a 'ou vaivai.
> Foa'i mai le mālosi ma.
> Fa'asino mai ou ala le suafa.
> o Iesu
> 'Āmene.[18]

SCENE SEVEN

Dream time Niue.

STORYTELLER: Fale kept living for her children and, of course, her husband, who was always able to make it up to her somehow. She loved him. She loved him a lot.

No one ever smacked or yelled at the children; she protected them from the interfering aunties.

The women in the village feared her independence: Fale claimed it.

Taniela's family were always trying to tell him to control his wife. But he had learnt from the first time not to take their advice. He knew a man left his family for his wife and children. That included leaving advice from his mother and sisters.

TANIELA: Fale, there is word your mother is sick ... She wants

---

[18] Thank you Lord for my life
Thank you Lord for the life of my family.
Forgive me for my sins and for those who sin against me.
Give me the strength to stand up when I am down.
Give me strength.
Show me your path.
In Jesus name
Amen.

you to return to Pago Pago.

Shhh…

Leave the children with me. You must go and see her. Take Ikinofo with you.

It's going to be all right.

FALE: The day arrived and I was standing on the deck of the *Tofua* with Ikinofo, waving to my family and husband.

SCENE EIGHT

Dream time Amerika Sāmoa.

LINDA: Good to be home, ah? Welcome back, my sister!

STORYTELLER: Giving away Michael at birth had affected everything that came afterward. The missing piece of her heart remained missing. And something else inside her went missing.

Somehow, in the mix of returning and not having the responsibility of six children and her husband, Fale got loose, very loose. So loose that she didn't return for one month, or six months. Almost two years passed before she could be contacted by Taniela.

Those two years away went fast for Fale. It was an eternity for the children back in Niue.

Taniela's brothers had moved to New Zealand.

TONGA: New Zealand is the land of milk and honey.

Plenty jobs.

Plenty women.

Plenty good times.

Good education for the kids.

Don't need the visa.

No problem, just get your airfare!

STORYTELLER: Taniela made up his mind to move the children to New Zealand. He worked and saved hard.

He finally contacted Fale.

When he rang, she cried a million tears. She was sorry and filled with guilt.

Fale agreed to leave Sāmoa and reunite with the family in New Zealand.

LINDA: You must be crazy! You can't leave. You can't go back to that. Your life is better here. Fale, come with me to America.

STORYTELLER: One of either two things happened.

Story one: Her mother's sister was supposed to bring Ikinofo to the airport that afternoon, but didn't show. She got on the plane without him.

Story two: Fale's mother asked her to leave Ikinofo. Fale agreed without talking to Taniela.

Whatever story was true, Fale carried the guilt all the way to New Zealand. When she arrived at the Auckland airport with no Ikinofo, Taniela cried. She couldn't explain.

It was 1972: the era of the dawn raids in Auckland. For years, the pigs broke into overcrowded houses in the early hours; arresting Polynesian families, putting them in jails, sending them back to where they came from.

The overwhelming support of the indigenous peoples, the Māoris, sprung into place. They protested against the dawn raids on their cousins from the South Pacific. The migration of the Māoris to Aotearoa New Zealand, Land of the Long White Cloud, can be traced by the navigation of waka through the South Pacific Ocean. Our indigenous cousins fought for us to stay on their islands.

Māori movements are used for this chant.

(Māori waiata)

Ehara i te mea
Nō nāianei te aroha
Nō ngā tūpuna
I tuku iho
I tuku iho.[19]

STORYTELLER: Fale rushed to hug her children, but none of them responded.

They stood blank with empty bodies when she embraced them.

They didn't want her anymore.

SCENE NINE

STORYTELLER: A year passed by, it was 1973 ...

TIEN: I was born at National Women's Hospital. My mother's tubes were tied and my father named me 'Theend'. Number seven for Taniela, number eight for Fale.

I hated being the youngest in my family. My sisters didn't like my mum. I didn't like my sisters. They were mean and always teased me.

In my opinion, the youngest always gets the brunt of the family shit and is always the strongest for it.

In their opinion, I was spoilt.

Jealousy. That's what my dad always said.

'They just jealous.' Shame about that.

---

[19] Love and understanding are not
Recent emotions
They were things handed down by
Our ancestors
Our ancestors.

I loved my mother. I remember waking up in the twilight morning cuddling up to her back. We'd walk to catch the 6am train to New Lynn, where she worked in a factory making plates and cups. I went to day care right across the road. She'd buy me little sticks of chewing gum, Twisties, chocolate and a Spaceman bottle drink.

We lived in Sunnyvale, in a big blue house mounted on a hill. Behind it was a valley of cows and horses. Dad had made an umu pit to cook food. Mum maintained the garden with taro, bananas, peas, carrots, cabbages and radishes. We had big peach trees and apple trees in the back. Heaps of food to pick on while playing on the steep, green hill, and a side of lamb in the fridge. Not like Niue or Sāmoa.

In those early years of Fale being in New Zealand, and as soon as I could speak, I was her voice and ears. I was never allowed to speak Niuean or Sāmoan. Only English.

I was afraid of my siblings, not because they teased me, but because they treated Mum differently and I couldn't understand why.

FALE: I am 35 years old. I work in the factory. Five years I stay here. Six children here. Two children lost. Husband drink too much. But I like this place Niu Sila. It's a beautiful!

TIEN: When it came to my turn of Mum abandoning me, I crumbled.

When I was sick, she would come home and take care of me. So I pretended to be sick a lot.

One day, she finally took me with her. A small flat on K Road. It was the red-light district in Auckland where the Pacific islanders drank.

STORYTELLER: Pub was called The Rising Sun. Mum's flat was on top of a fish shop that looked directly into the pub. Fale wasn't a drinker or a smoker. She sold her tote tickets there.

FALE: Buy one ticket, $2: win $100!

TIEN: She had to be smart to survive without an income.

She found the famous Niue leaf polo that grew in the swamp areas around Auckland. We'd find a patch and collect it into big plastic bags. She'd sell it to Polynesian food stores and cook it for her friends. Problem was, it was always next to the bloody motorway.

STORYTELLER: Fale became known as a fofō practitioner, healing with her hands. Many parents would bring their children for her to heal.

Fale had truly moved out from her family, husband and home.

She moved in with ... Joe, was his name, for three years. After that it was Ben.

TIEN: I realised over time he was her friend. Her partner. Her own saviour.

SCENE TEN

Dream time New Zealand.

STORYTELLER: Fale had developed diabetes over the years and, depending on who took her to the doctors, she would come back with bags full of white medicine.

FALE: I don't like it! It's yukky! Get away! Get out!

STORYTELLER: She reached menopause early and was very emotional. The children took her to the doctors and they prescribed anti-depressants, diabetes pills, blood pressure pills, heart pills, painkiller pills, anti-inflammatory pills, ear drops, eye drops, vaginal cream, anal cream – every fucking thing you could imagine. It all ate away at her internal and external organs slowly.

'Family portrait' projection fades up on back wall.

TIEN: We, her children, thinking we knew better, labelled her 'mental'.

Mental because she didn't raise us properly.

Mental because she kept leaving.

Mental because she had a lover.

Mental because she left our father.

Mental because our father told us she was.

STORYTELLER: Post-natal depression, repressed childhood trauma, abandonment issues, bipolar disorder, depression, battered woman syndrome ... To Fale, none of these words meant anything.

Fale saw her children have children; her children's children have children. Her children graduate from universities, bible colleges. She saw the wealth of each one and was always so proud.

Projection fades out.

SCENE ELEVEN

Dream time New Zealand.

Fale and Tien are sitting watching TV.

FALE: I been talking with my friend.

TIEN: That's good.

FALE: In Amerika Sāmoa.

TIEN: Oh, do you still have friends there?

FALE: She said ... She said ...

TIEN: What did she say?

FALE: Never mind.

TIEN: Mum, hurry up!

FALE: They know where Ikinofo lives.

TIEN: Really?

FALE: Yes, with my mother in Seattle.

TIEN: Didn't she use to beat you like a dog?

FALE: 'O le Atua na te silafia mea 'uma.[20]

STORYTELLER: She flew out to Seattle to see her mother and hold Ikinofo in her arms again. The family flew him back to NZ to meet his brothers and sisters who were lost to him all his life.

Then in 2005 through talking to her friends on the phone in Auckland.

FALE: Tālofa Lava.[21]

'Ua mai oui?[22]

'O le ā?[23]

Michael? Michael?

'O e![24]

FALE cries out and drops to her knees crying.

I am 63 years old. I found my heart. Michael. I am lucky. Lucky, lucky. I got 7 children, 33 grandchildren and 2 great grandchildren now. Thank the lord. Fa'afetai, fa'afetai.

STORYTELLER: She found Michael. Still living in Amerika Sāmoa, in the village of Utu Lei, with his family. She brought him to New Zealand and introduced him to our family. Her heart was finally restored.

On April 12, 2006, after telling Ben on the phone to go pick the polo for her friend's birthday, in an emergency room at the Auckland Hospital, aged 64 ... Falemalama Abbey Reid ... died.

---

[20] God sees everything.
[21] Greetings
[22] How are you?
[23] What?
[24] You!

Forty-two movements are performed within a Sāmoan dance that represents the children, grandchildren and great-grandchildren of Falemalama.

SCENE TWELVE

Dream time Amerika Sāmoa.

FALE's voice can be heard singing Fa'afetai i le Atua.

FALE: Fa'afetai i le Atua
Le na tātou tupu ai
Ina 'ua na alofa fua
Iā te'i tatou uma
Ia pepese, Ia pepese
Aleluia fa'afetai
Aleluia fa'afetai.[25]

Sāmoan music is used for the taualunga.

Taualunga dance is performed by TIEN to finish the story.

---

[25] Give thanks to God
Who is our creator
For his never-ending love
For all of us
Sing, sing
Hallelujah thank you
Hallelujah thank you.

NEW ZEALAND PLAY SERIES FOUNDATION SUBSCRIBERS

THE FOLLOWING INDIVIDUALS AND ORGANISATIONS HAVE MADE A COMMITMENT TO NEW ZEALAND PLAY PUBLISHING BY PURCHASING THE FIRST TEN PLAYS IN THE NEW ZEALAND PLAY SERIES UPFRONT. WE THANK THEM FOR THEIR VITAL SUPPORT AND INVITE YOU TO JOIN THEM AS SUBSCRIBERS BY CONTACTING MARK AMERY AT DIRECTOR@PLAYMARKET.ORG.NZ, OR PHONE (04) 382 8462.

★★★★★★★★★★★★★★★★★★★★★★★★★★★★★★★★

- ALISTER MCDONALD
- ANDREW CAISLEY
- AUCKLAND CITY LIBRARY
- AUCKLAND THEATRE COMPANY
- BEVIN LINKHORN
- BRONWYN TWEDDLE
- CAMPBELL SMITH
- CONSTANCE KIRKCALDIE
- DANIELLE HODGSON
- DAVID JENKINS
- EMERGING ARTISTS TRUST
- HELEN AND DAVID ZWARTZ
- HON JUDITH TIZARD
- JAMES GRIFFIN
- JO MACKAY
- JUDITH DALE
- LYNDEE-JANE RUTHERFORD
- LYNDA CHANWAI-EARLE
- MARC MAUFORT
- MASSIVE COMPANY
- NOLA MILLER LIBRARY
- PALMERSTON NORTH CITY LIBRARY
- PETER HAMBLETON
- PROF CHRISTOPHER BALME
- PROF DAVID CARNEGIE
- RICHARD AND CHRISTINE AMERY
- ROGER HALL
- RUTH GRAHAM
- STEPHEN SINCLAIR
- STUART STRACHAN
- THE COURT THEATRE TRUST
- UNIVERSITY OF OTAGO LIBRARY
- WELLINGTON CITY LIBRARIES

★★★★★★★★★★★★★★★★★★★★★★★★★★★★★★★★